I0485138

Ancient Arbor

The Art of Clovis C.M.

Portraits

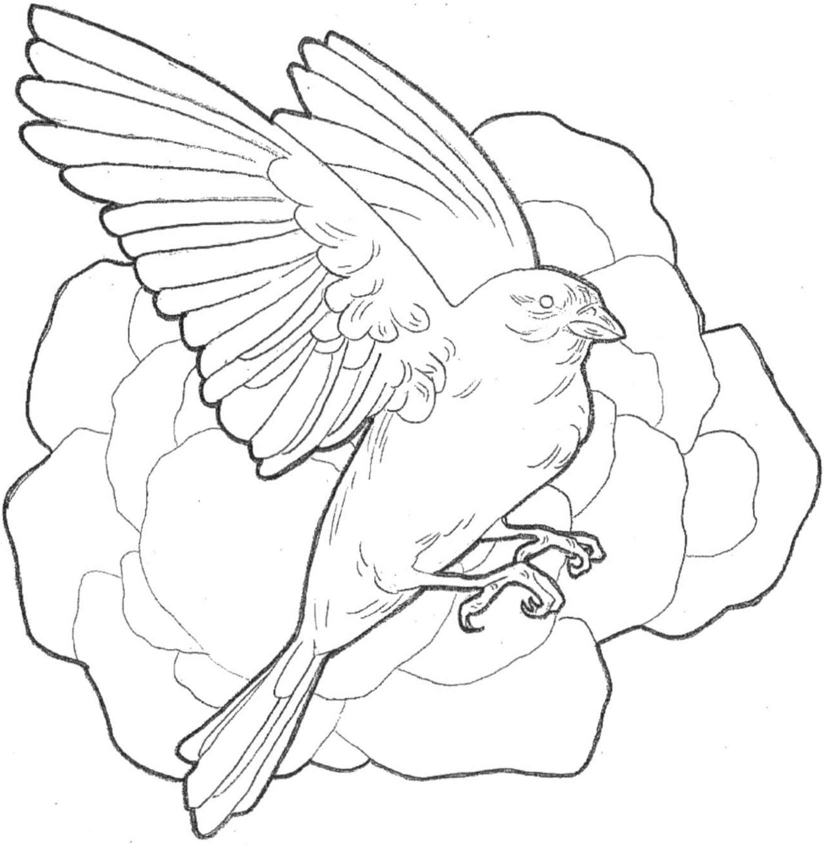

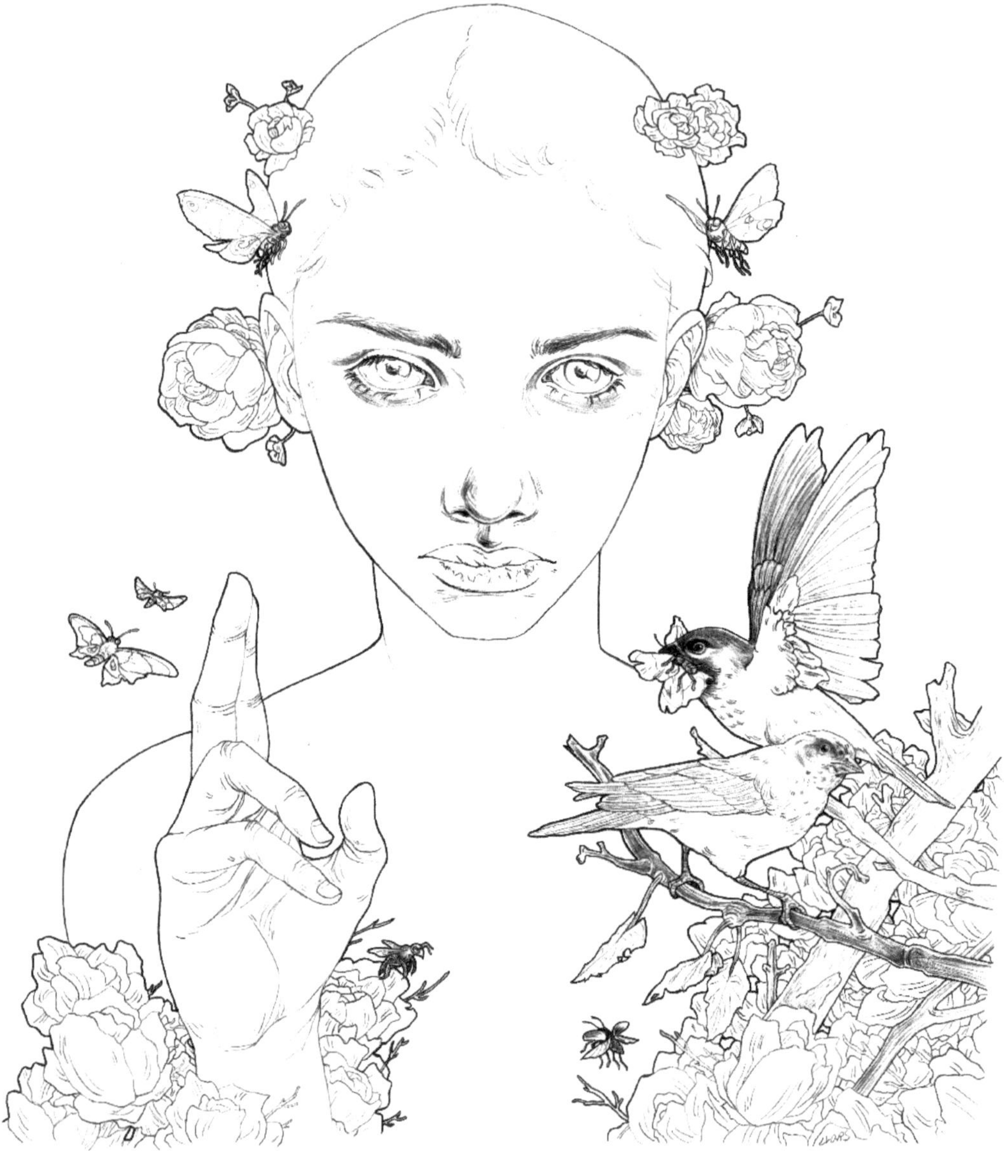

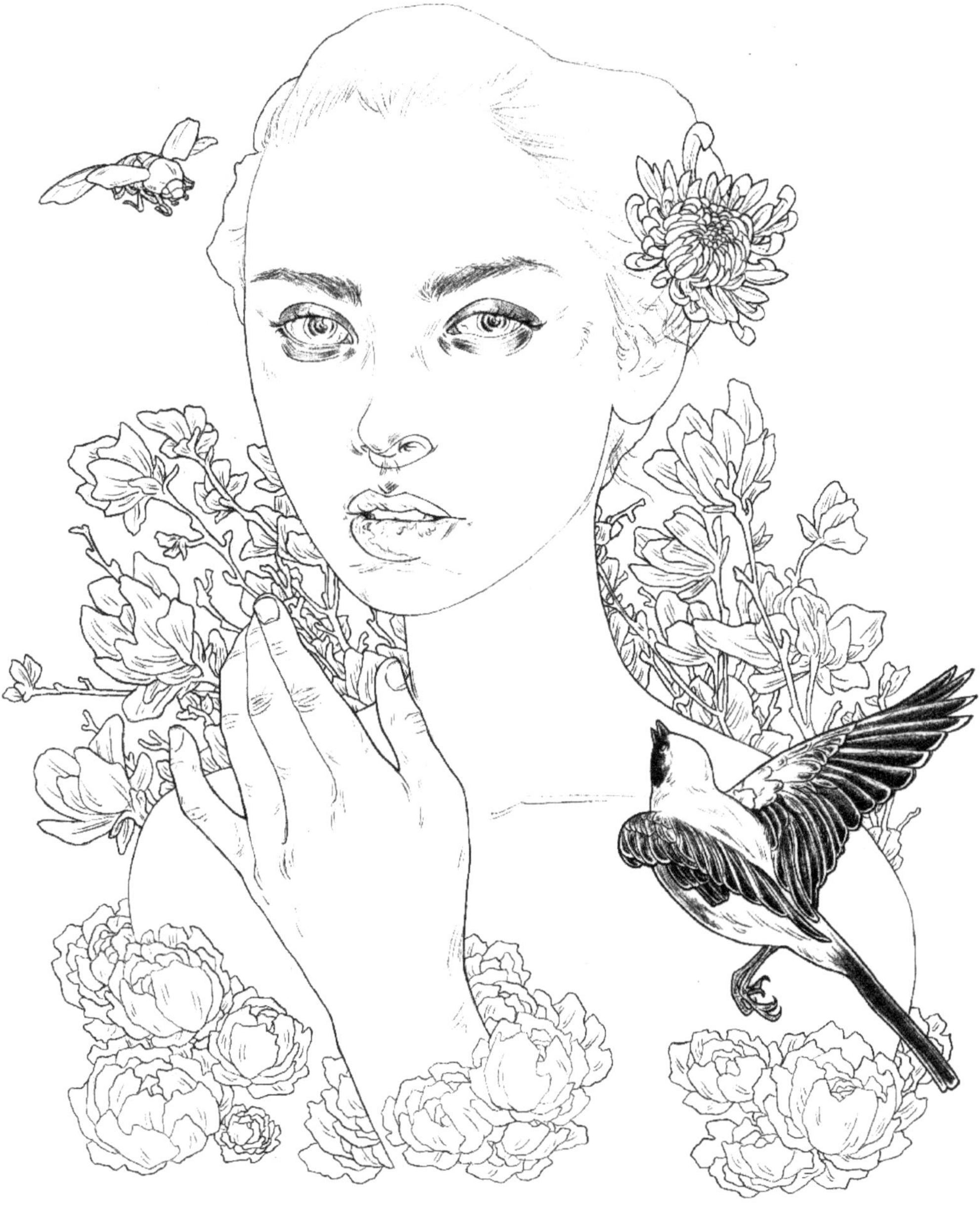

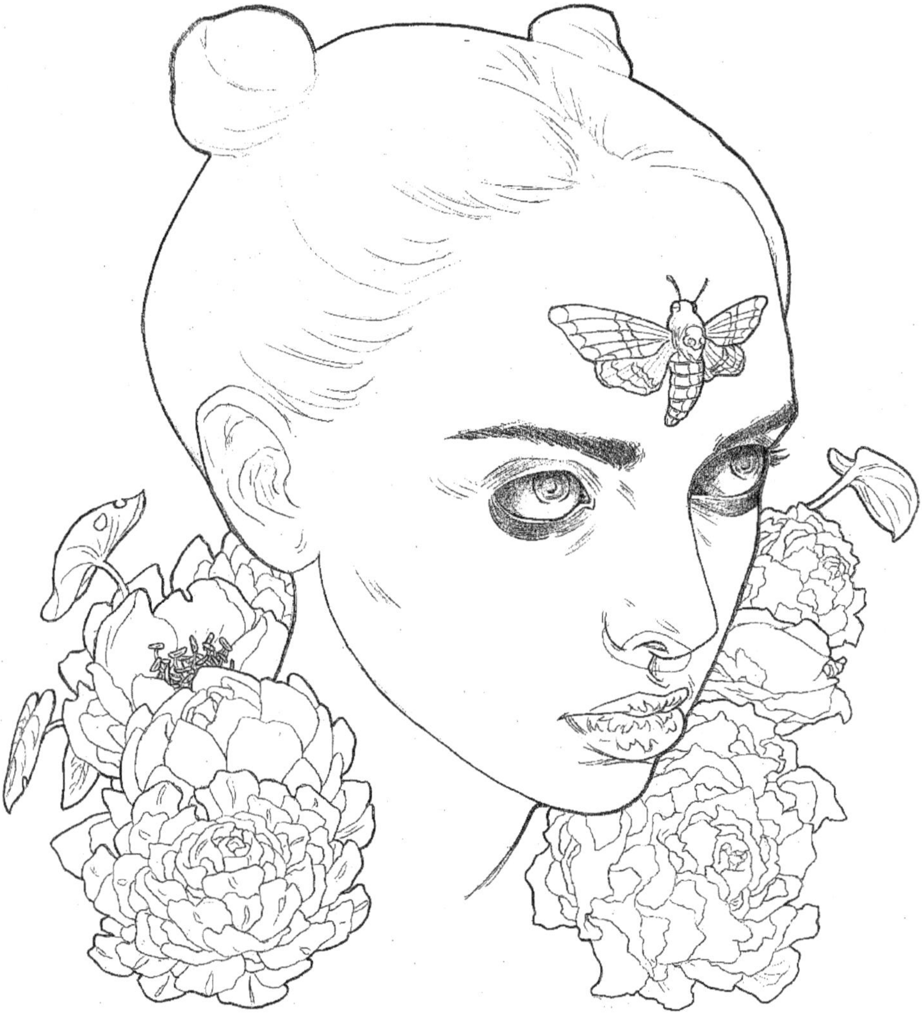

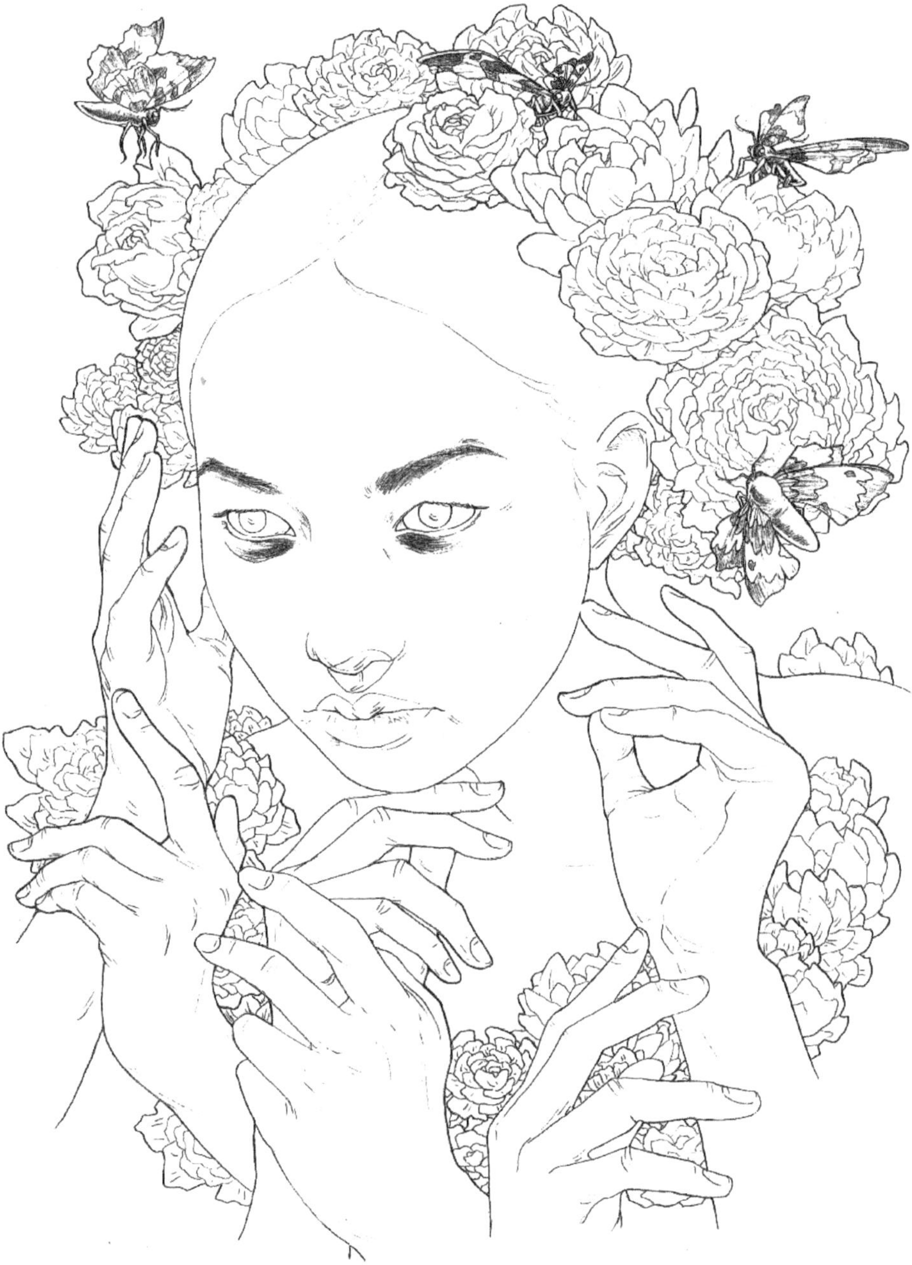

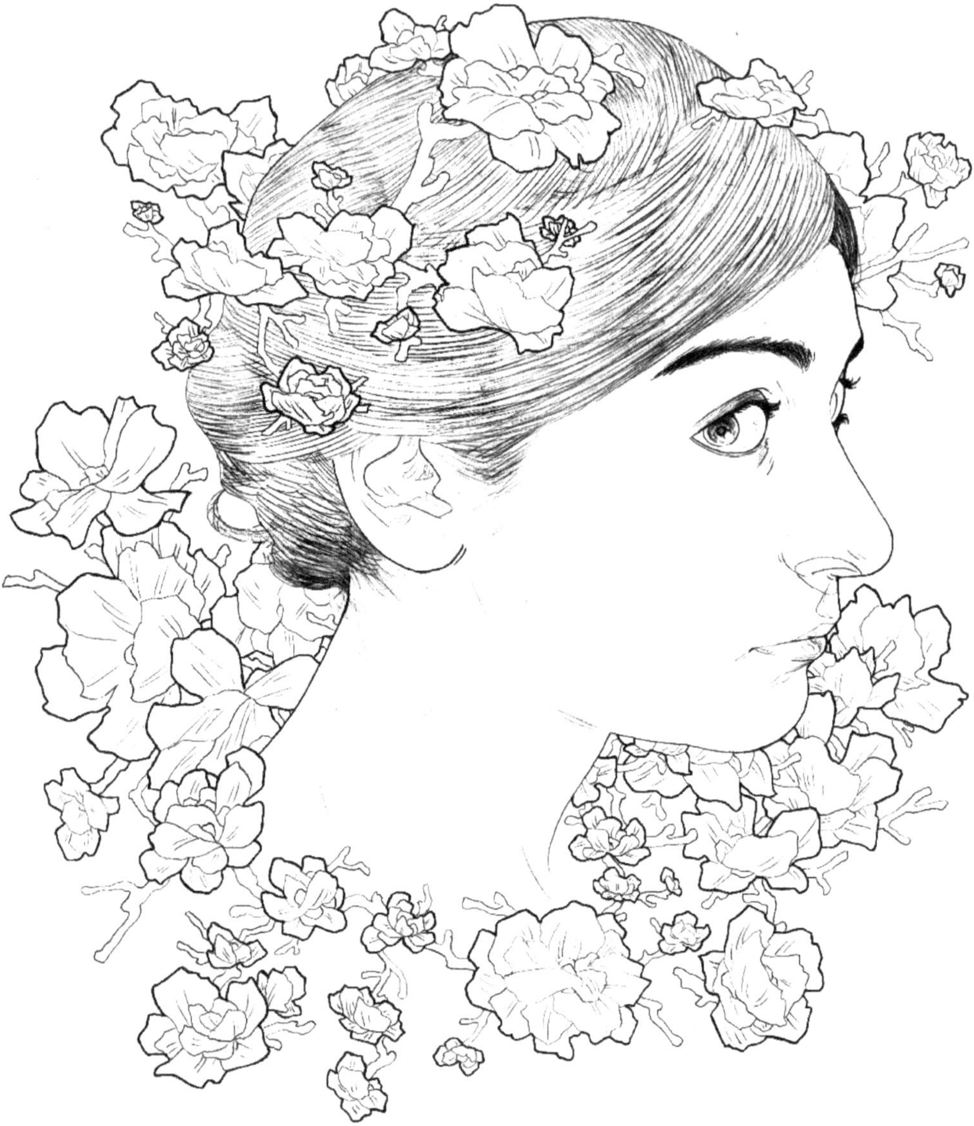

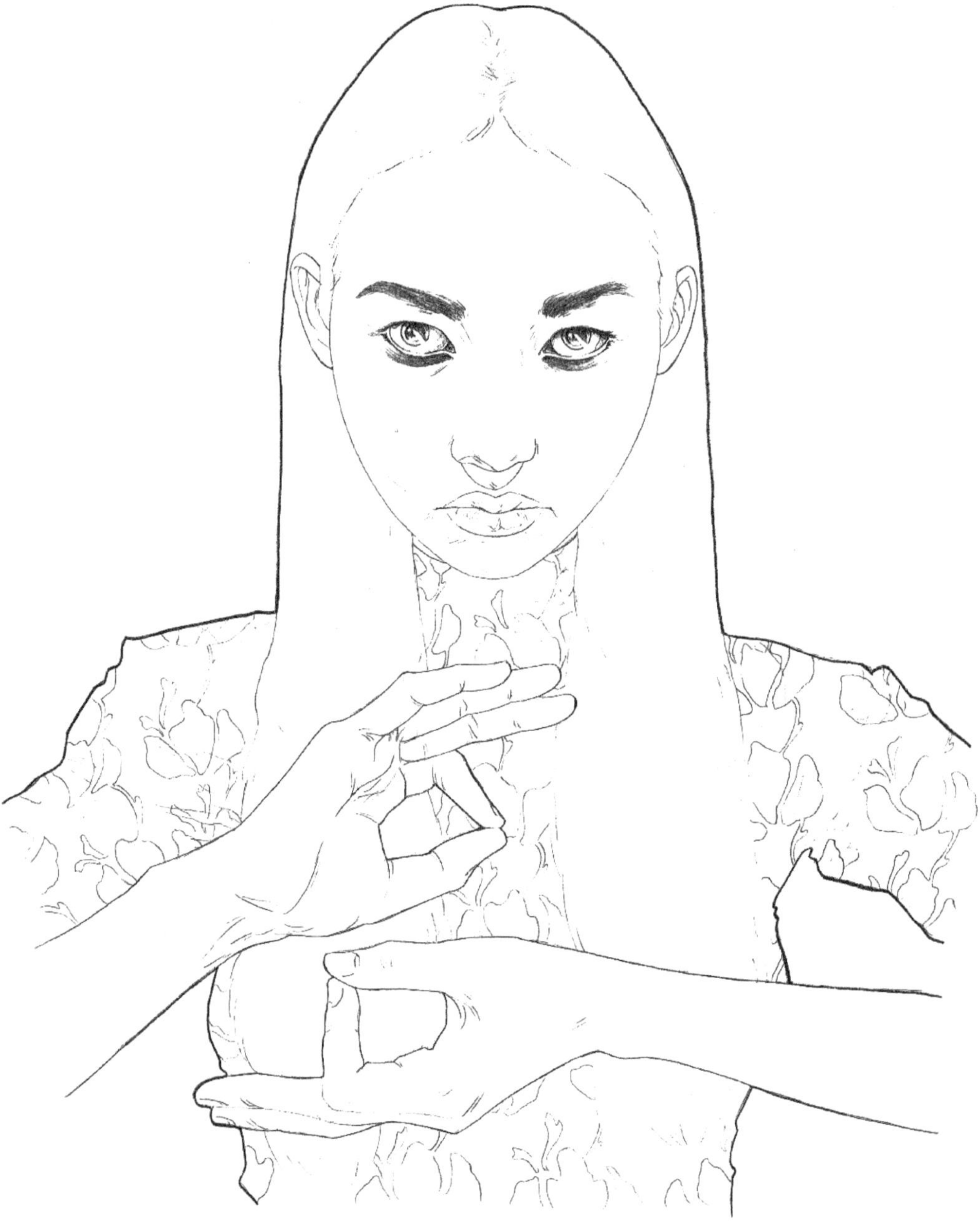

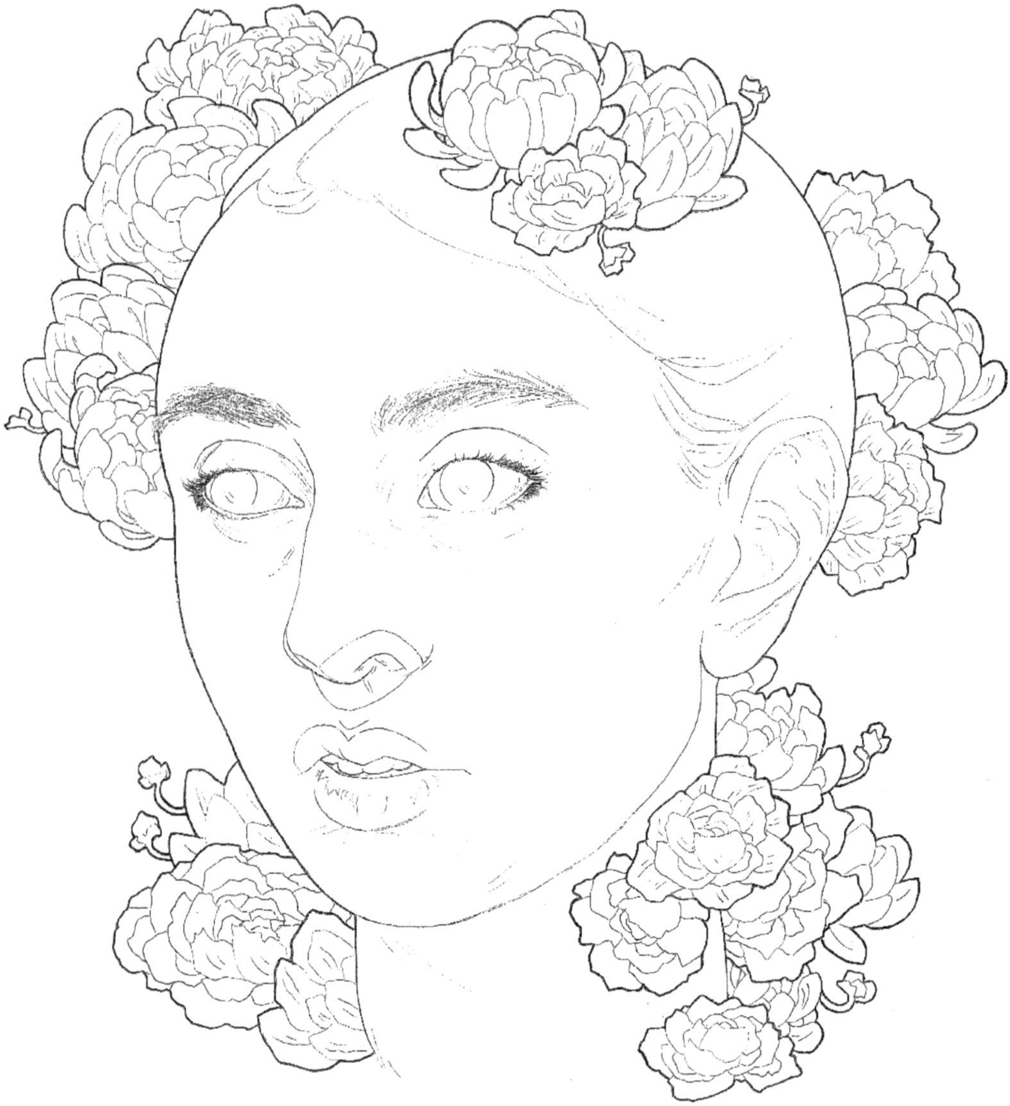

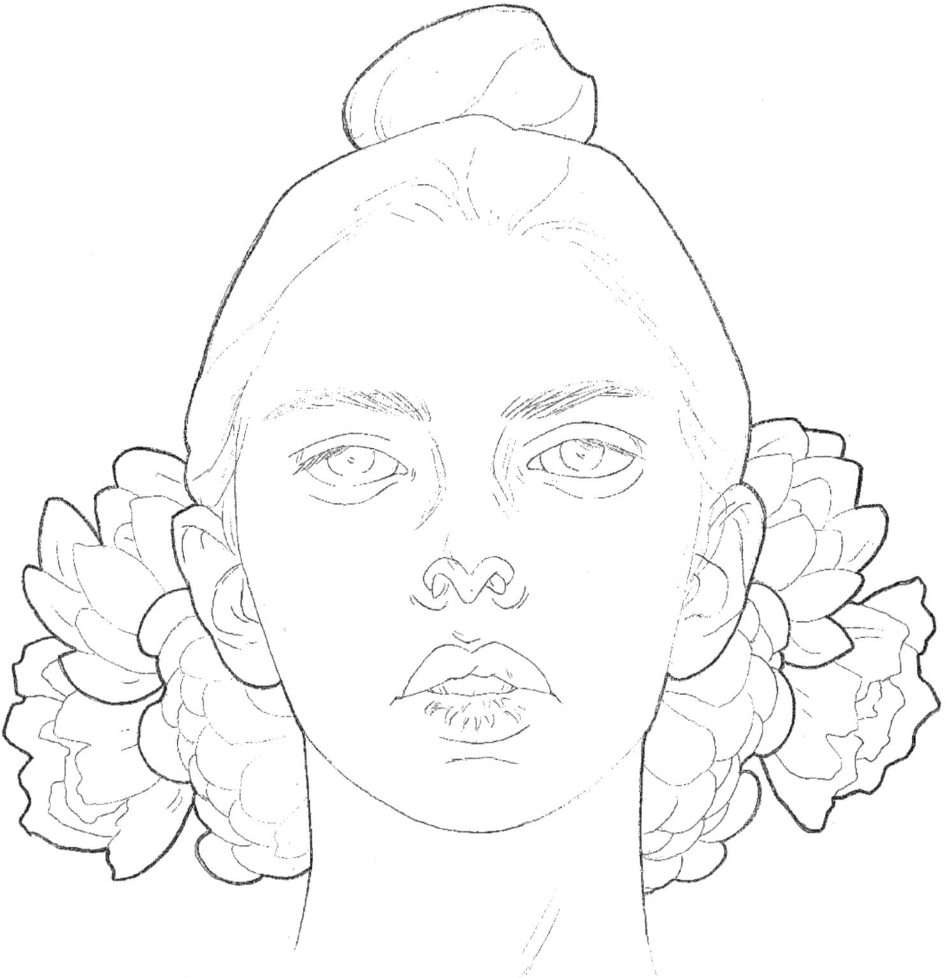

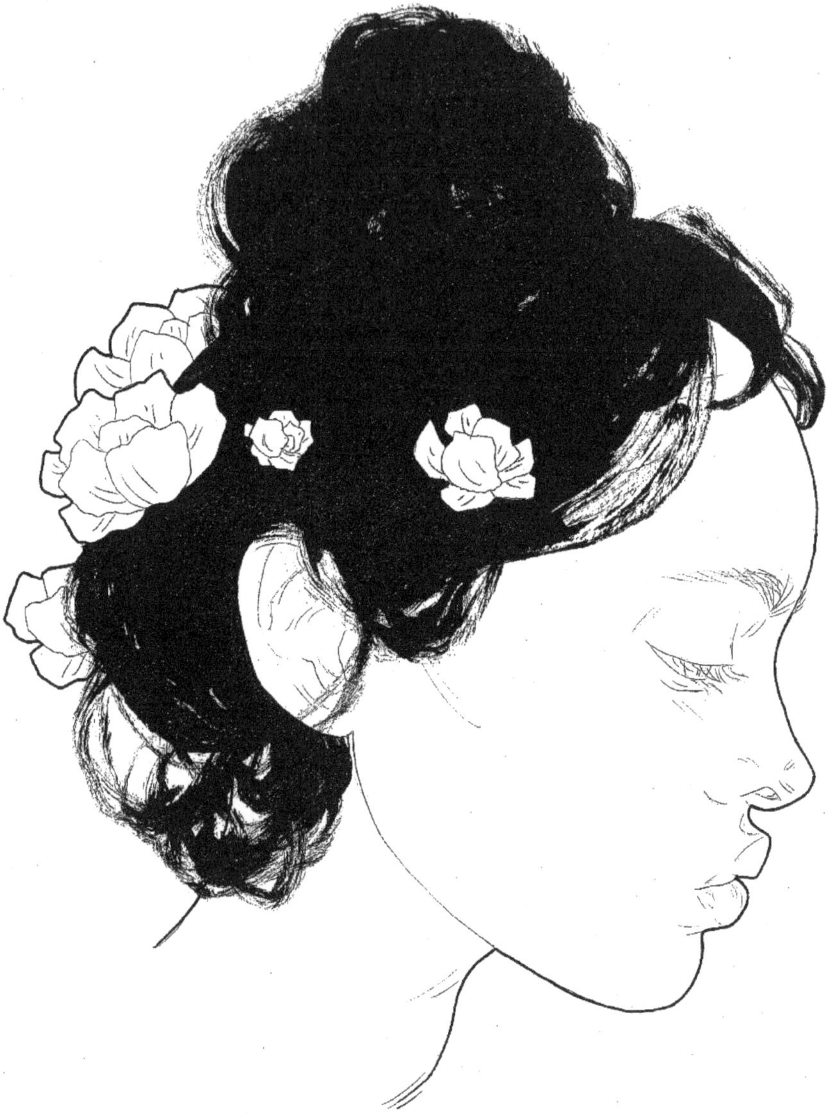

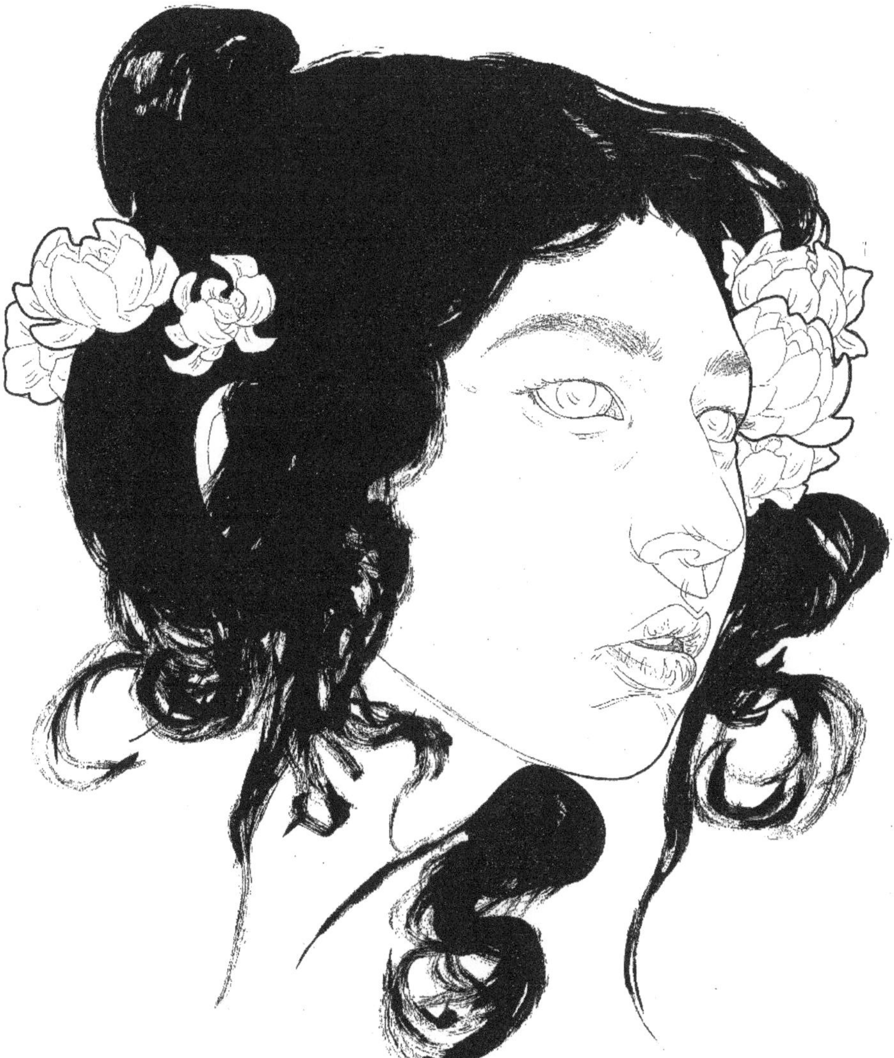

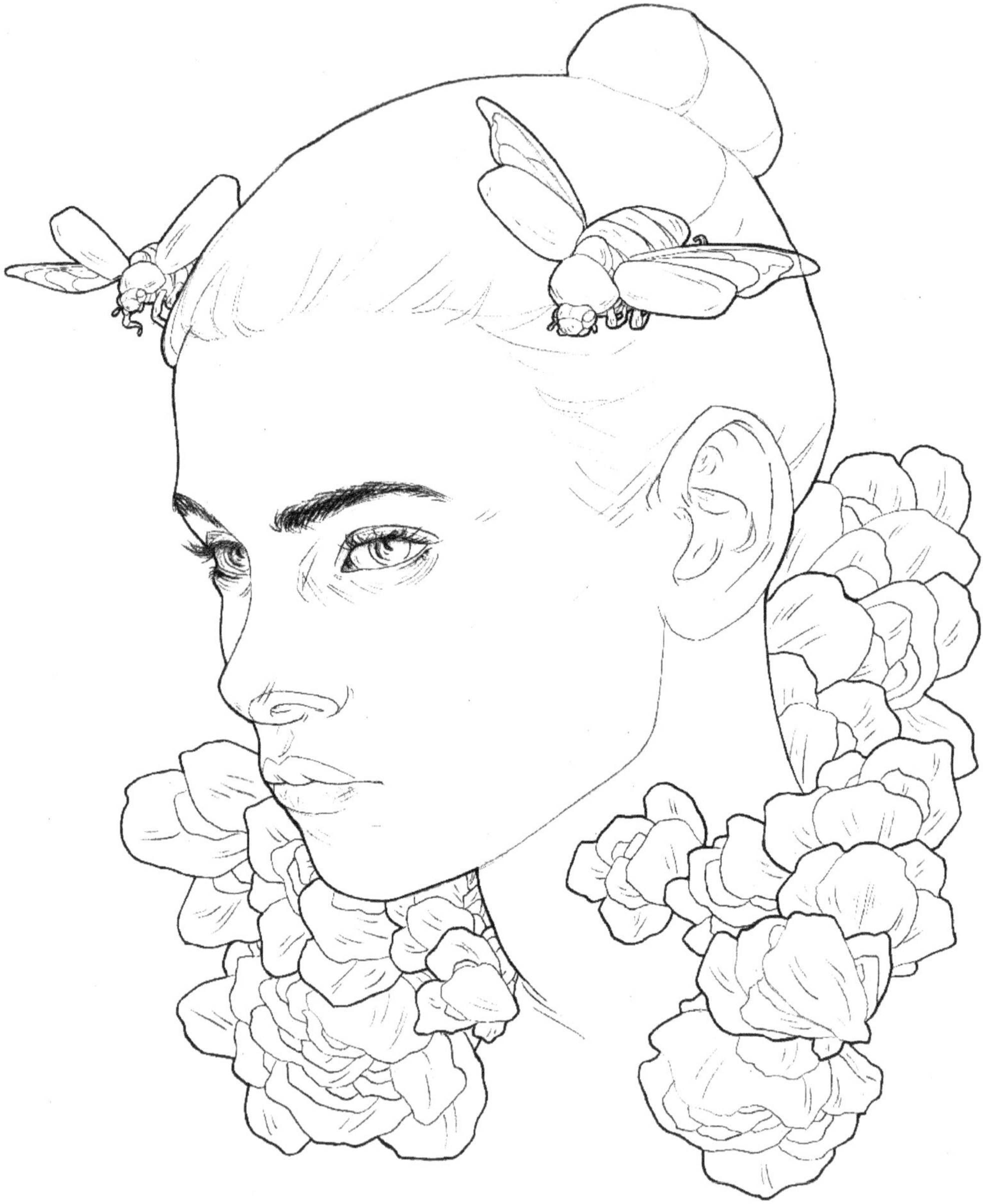

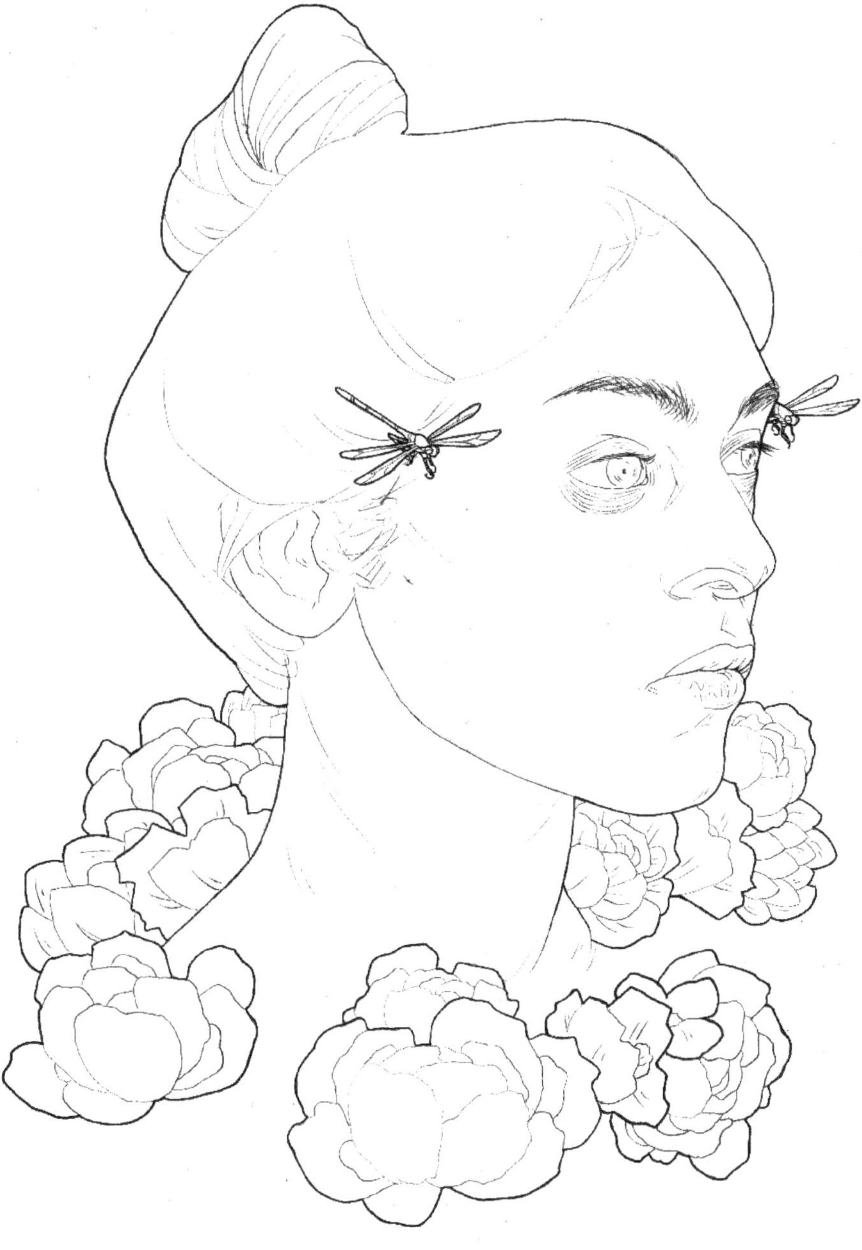

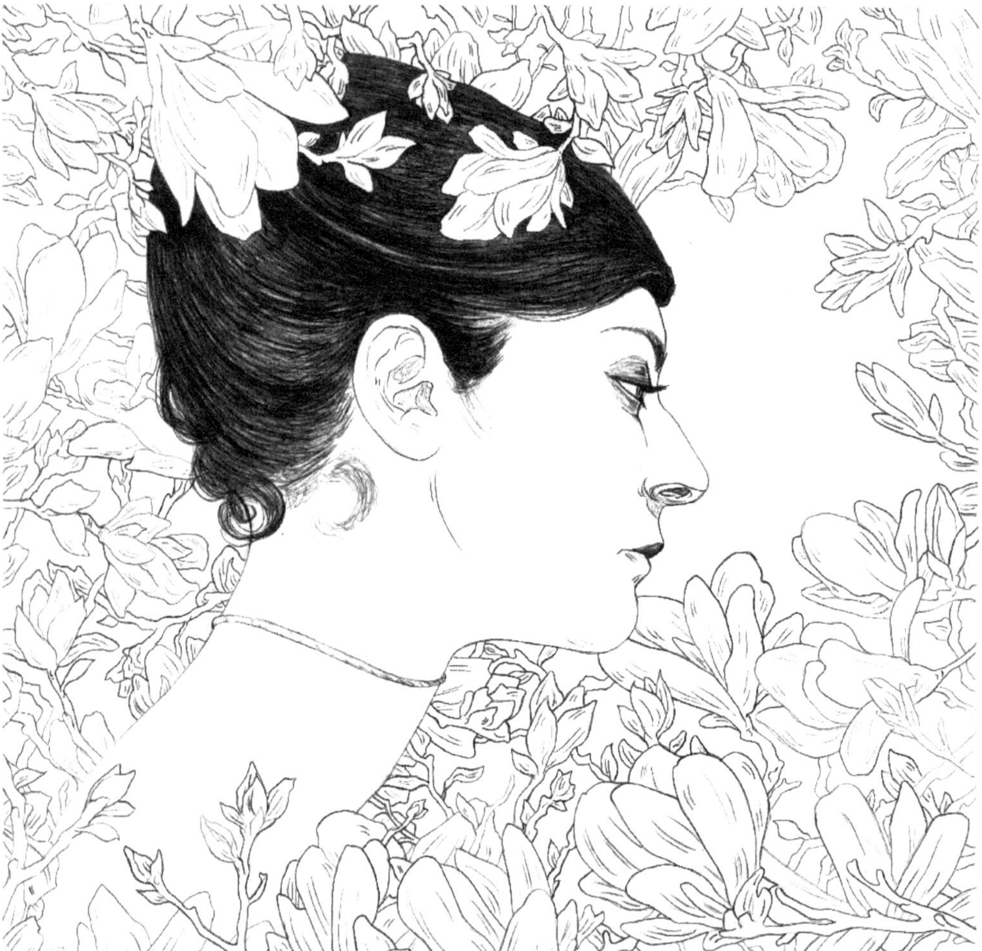

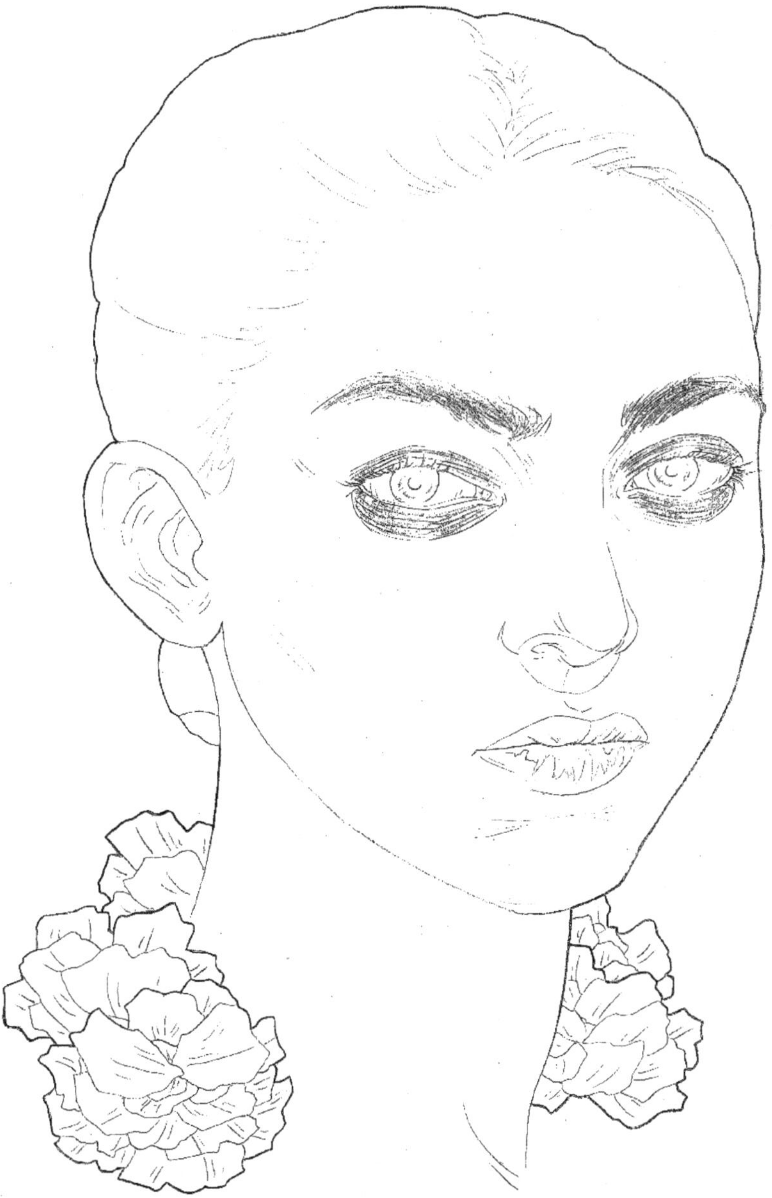

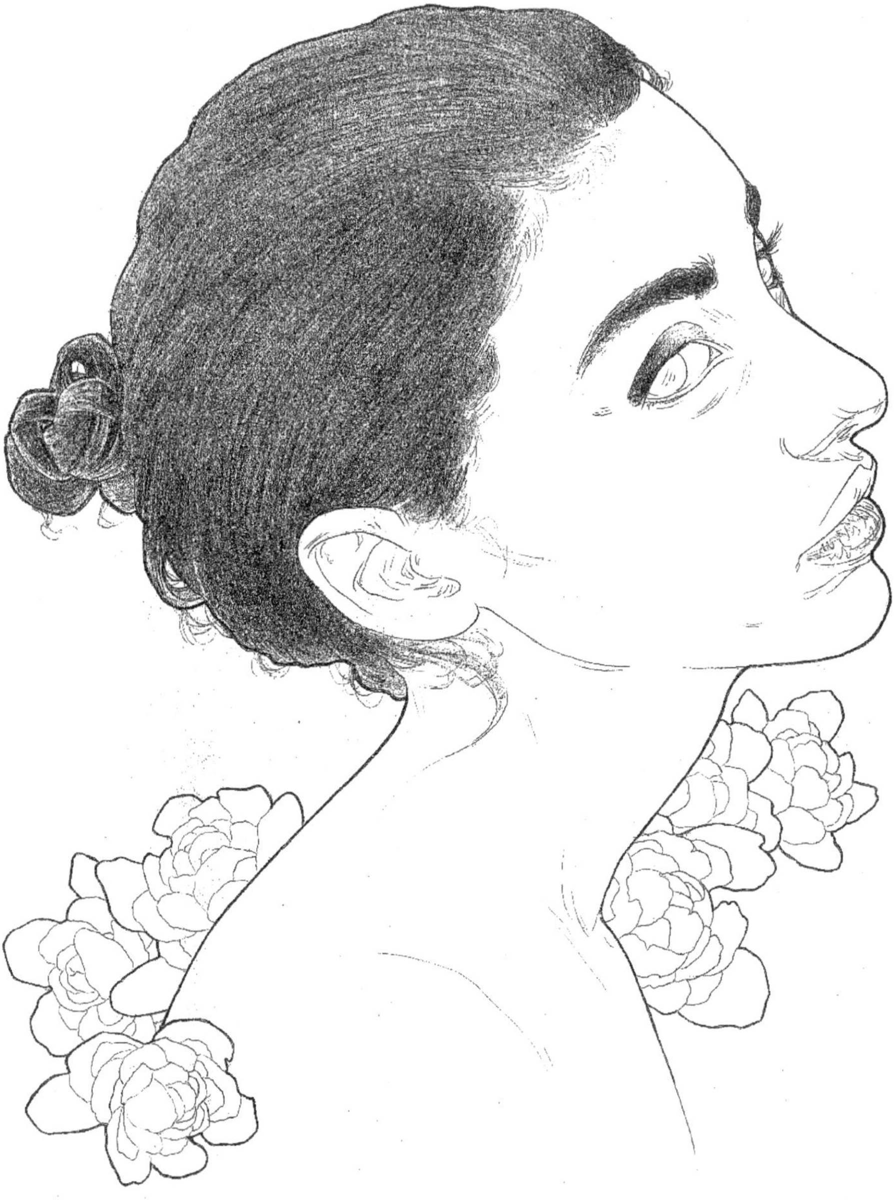

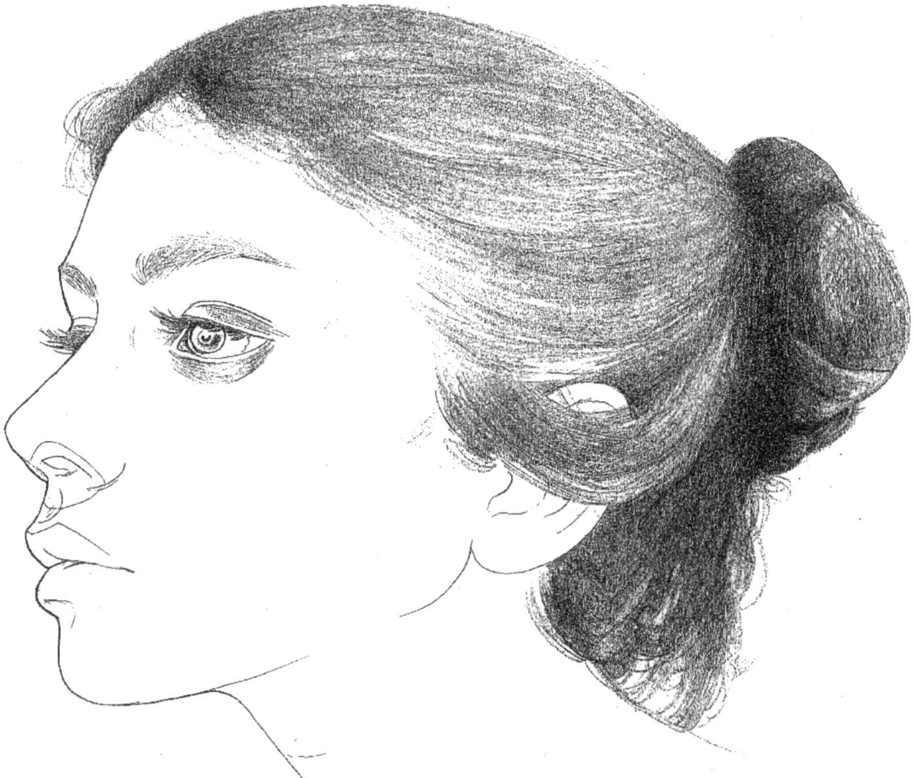

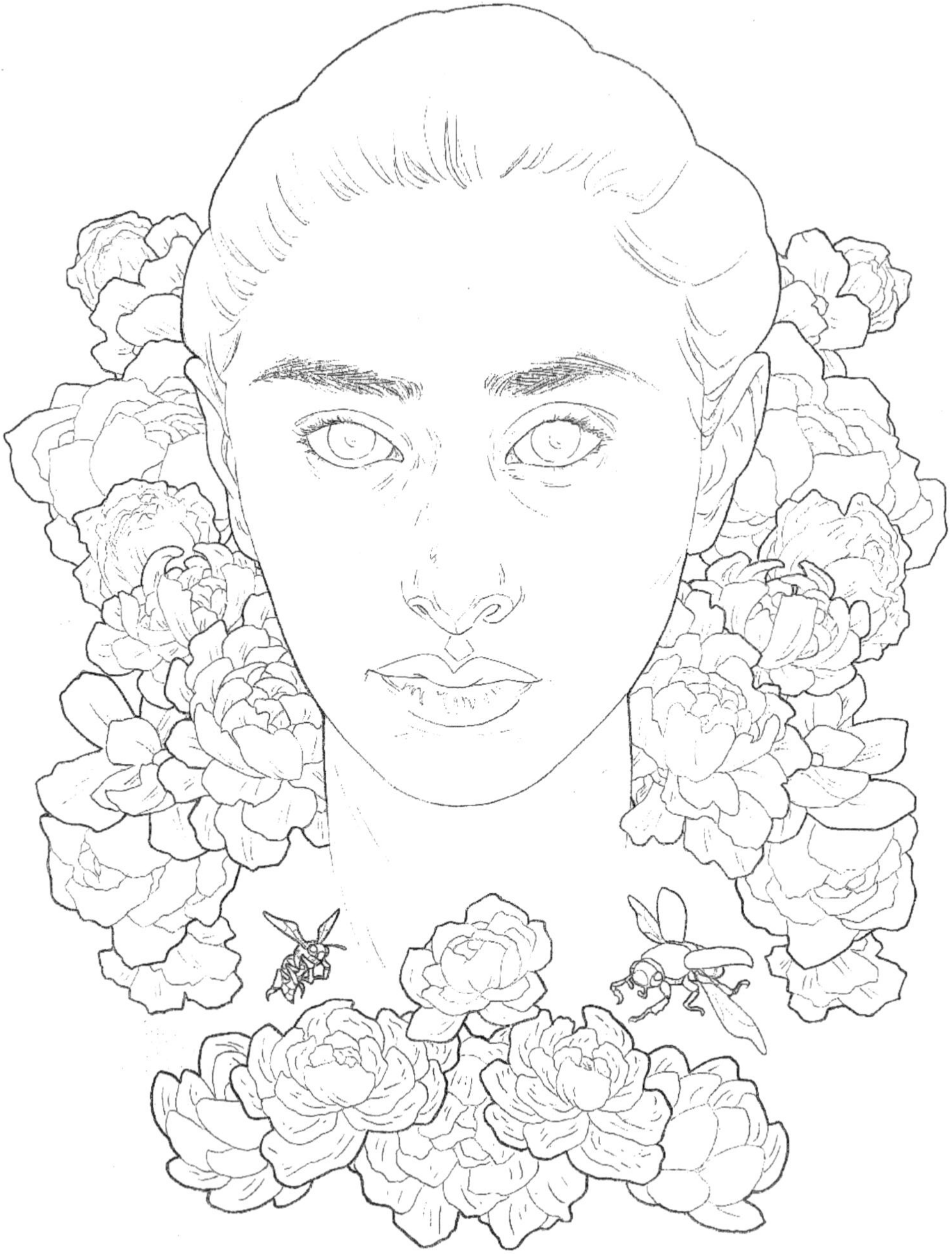

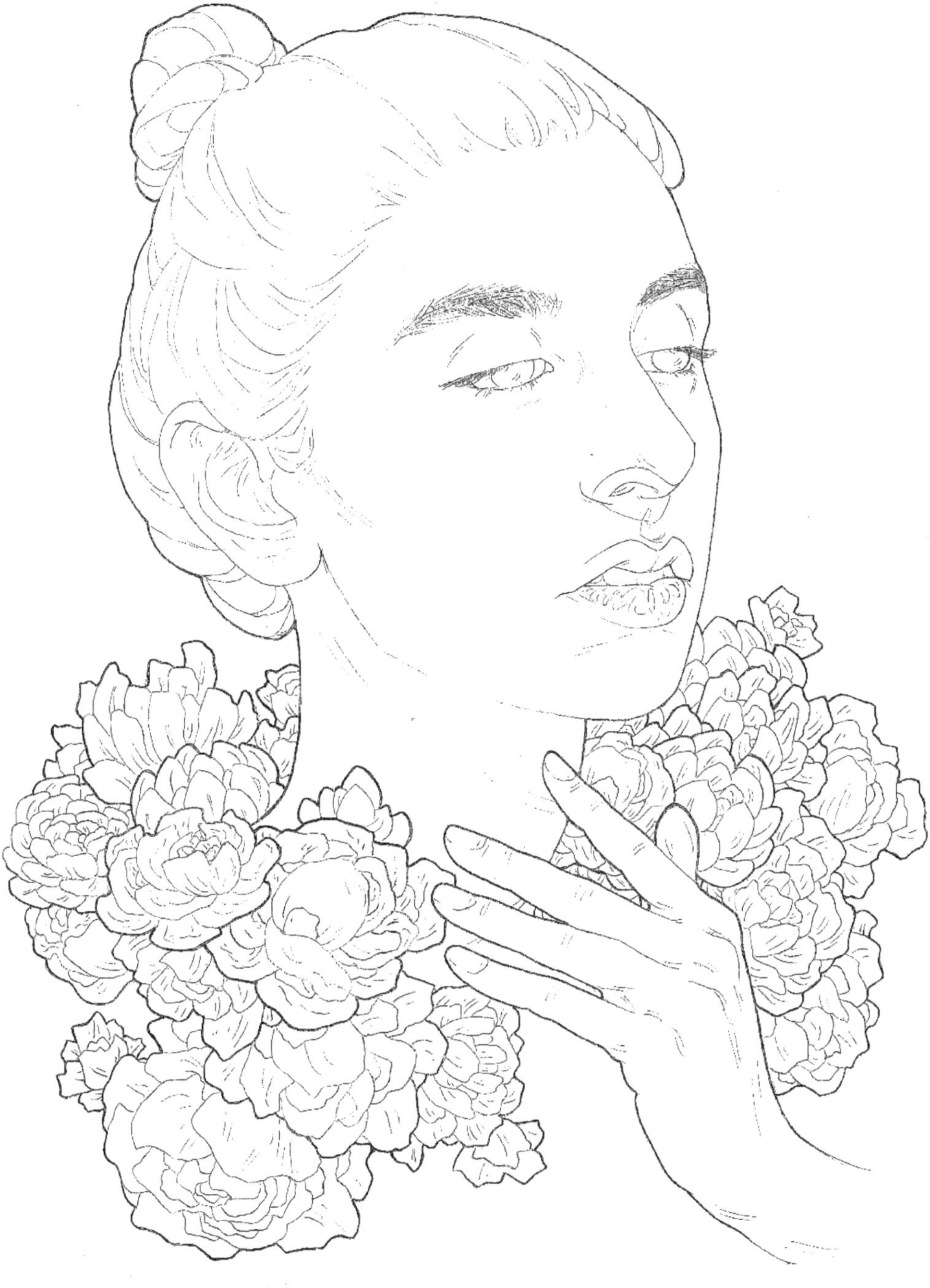

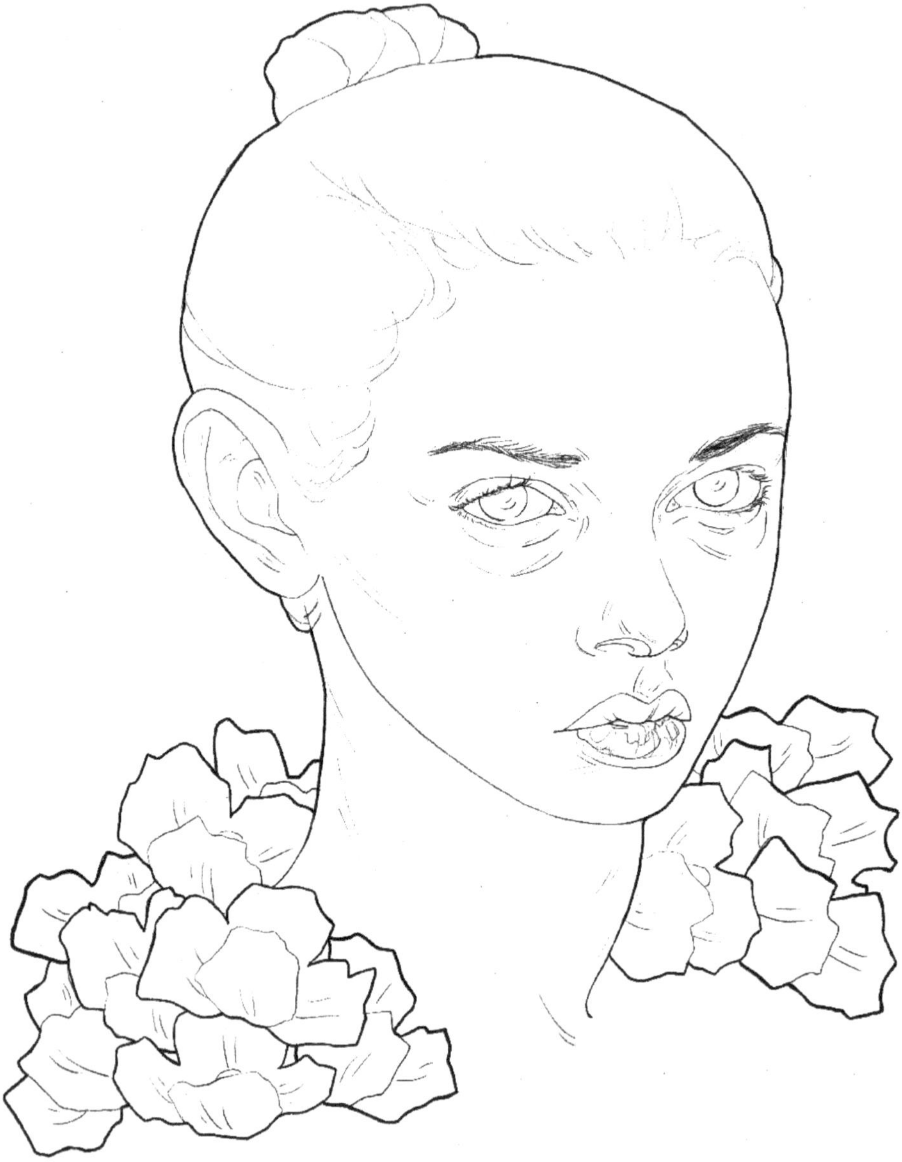

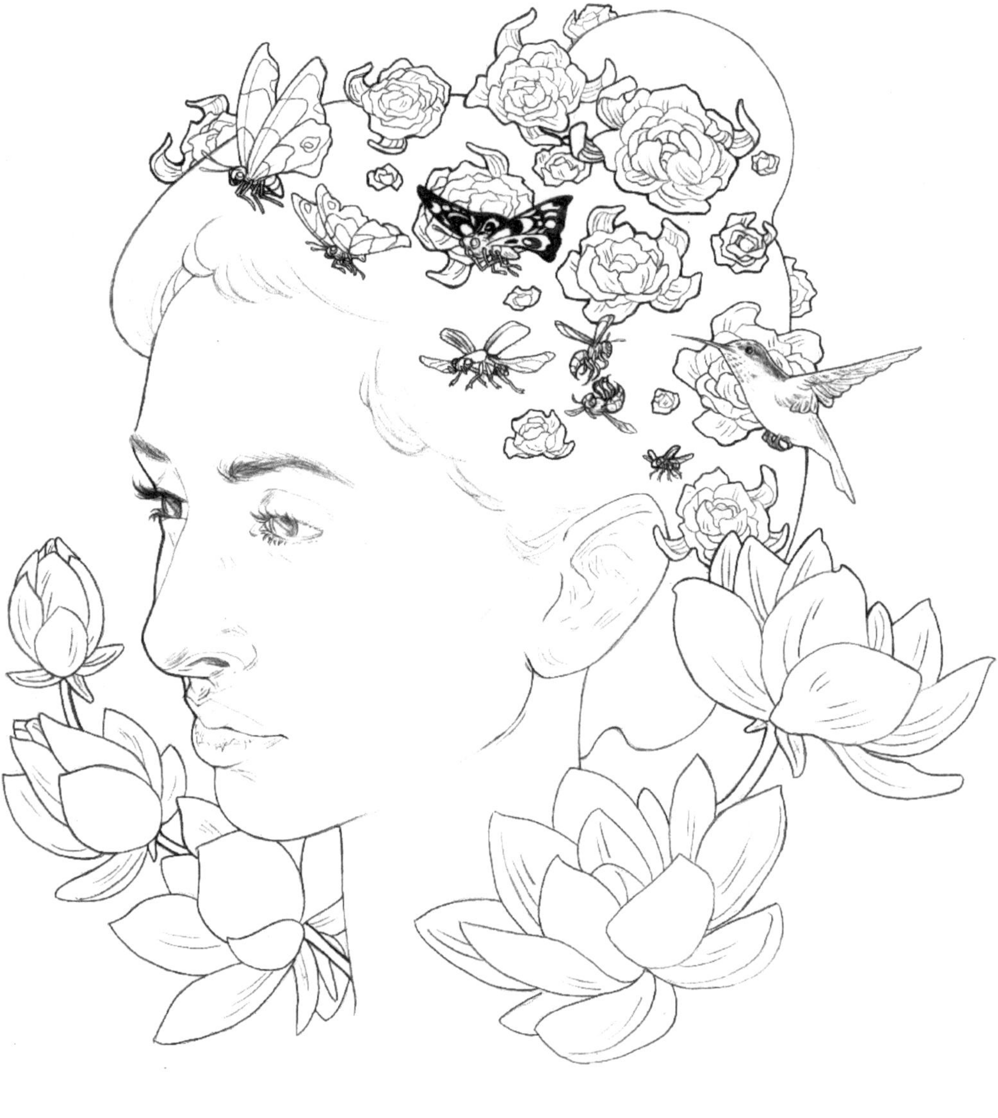

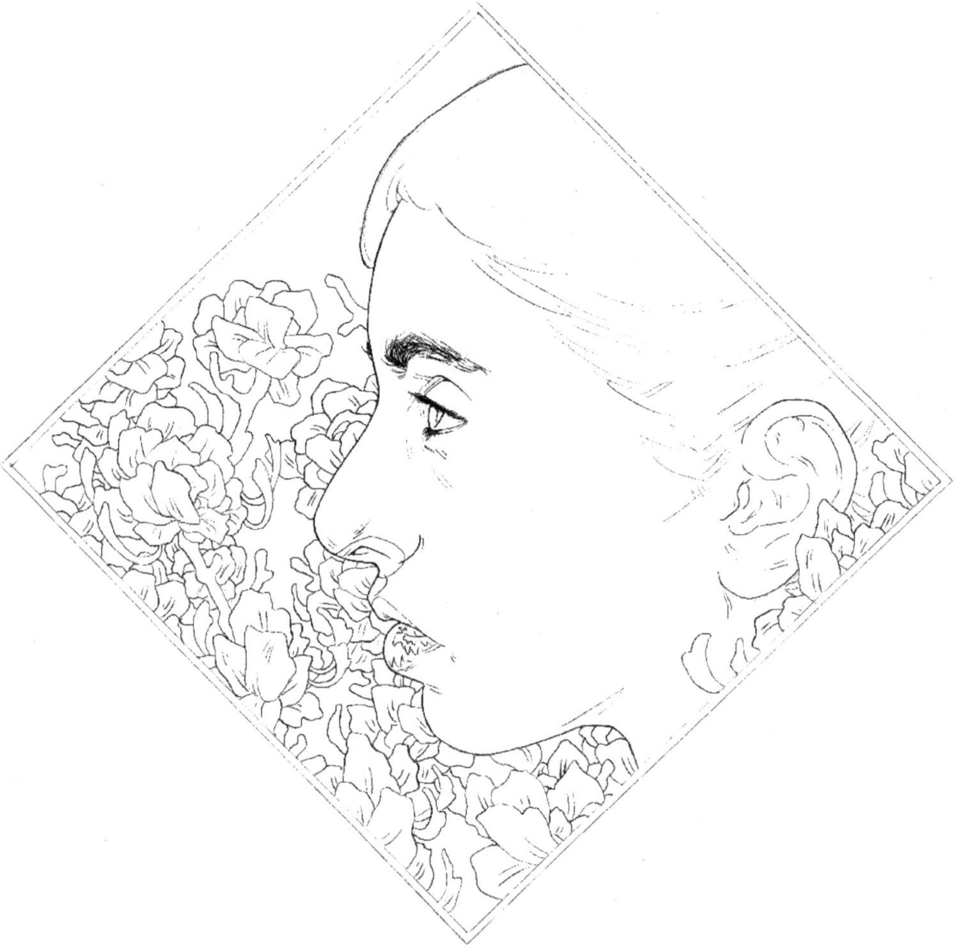

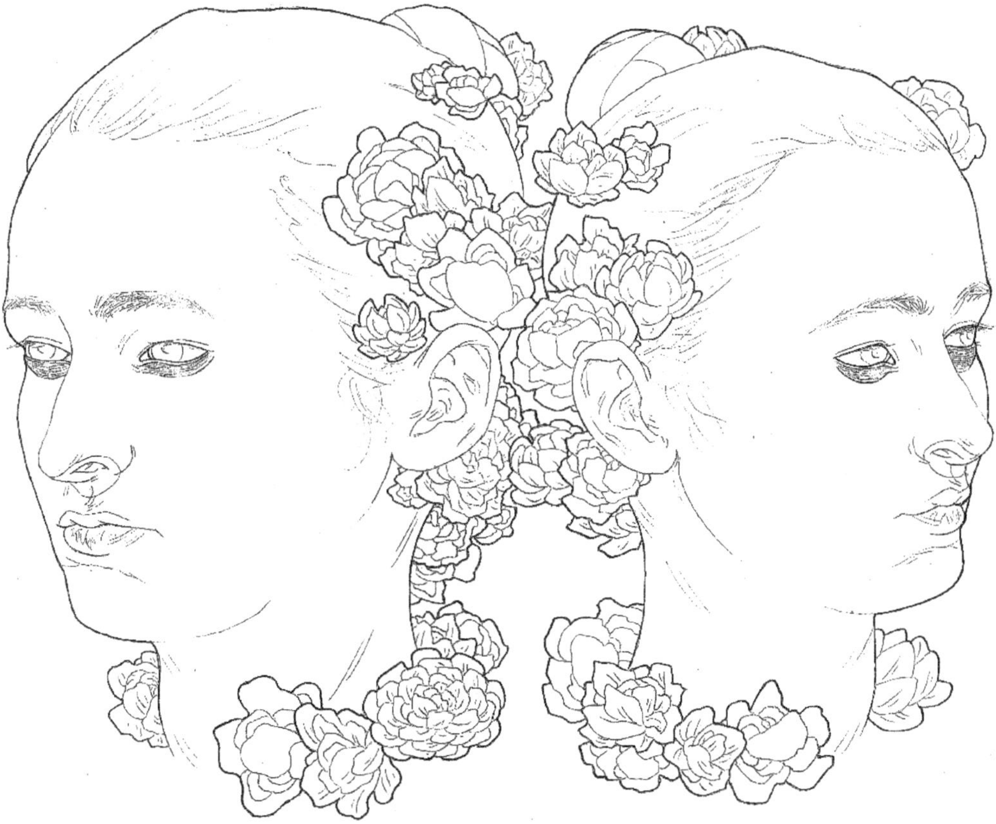

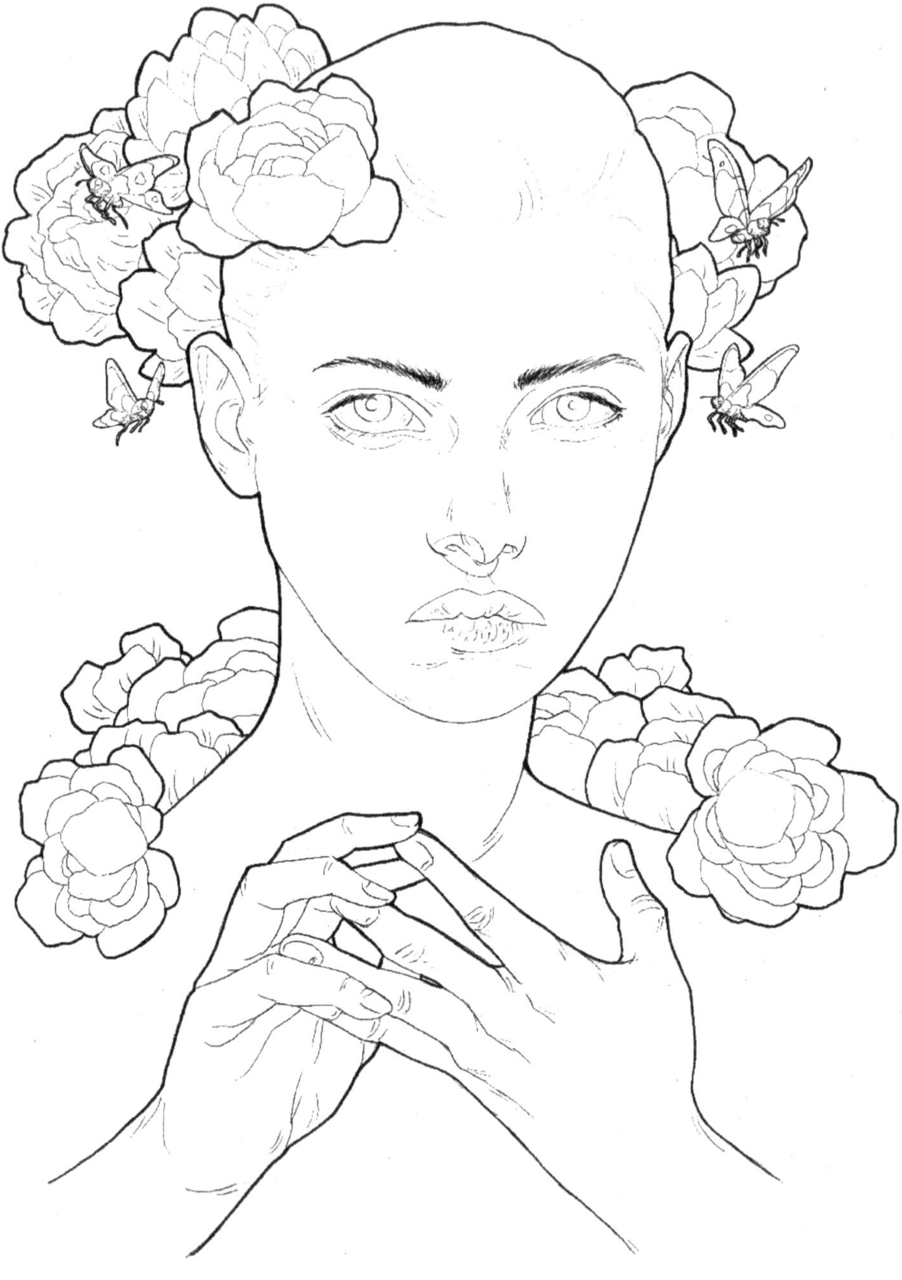

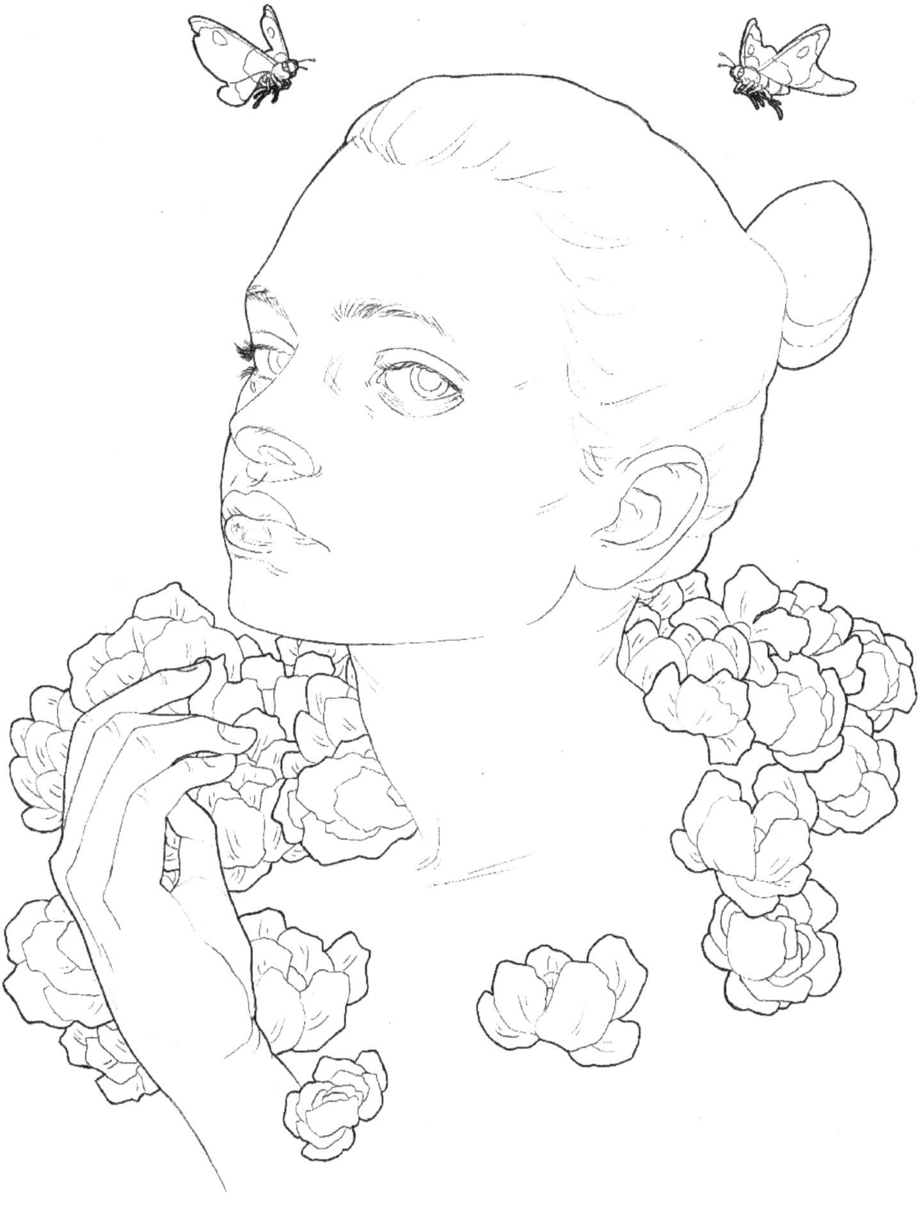

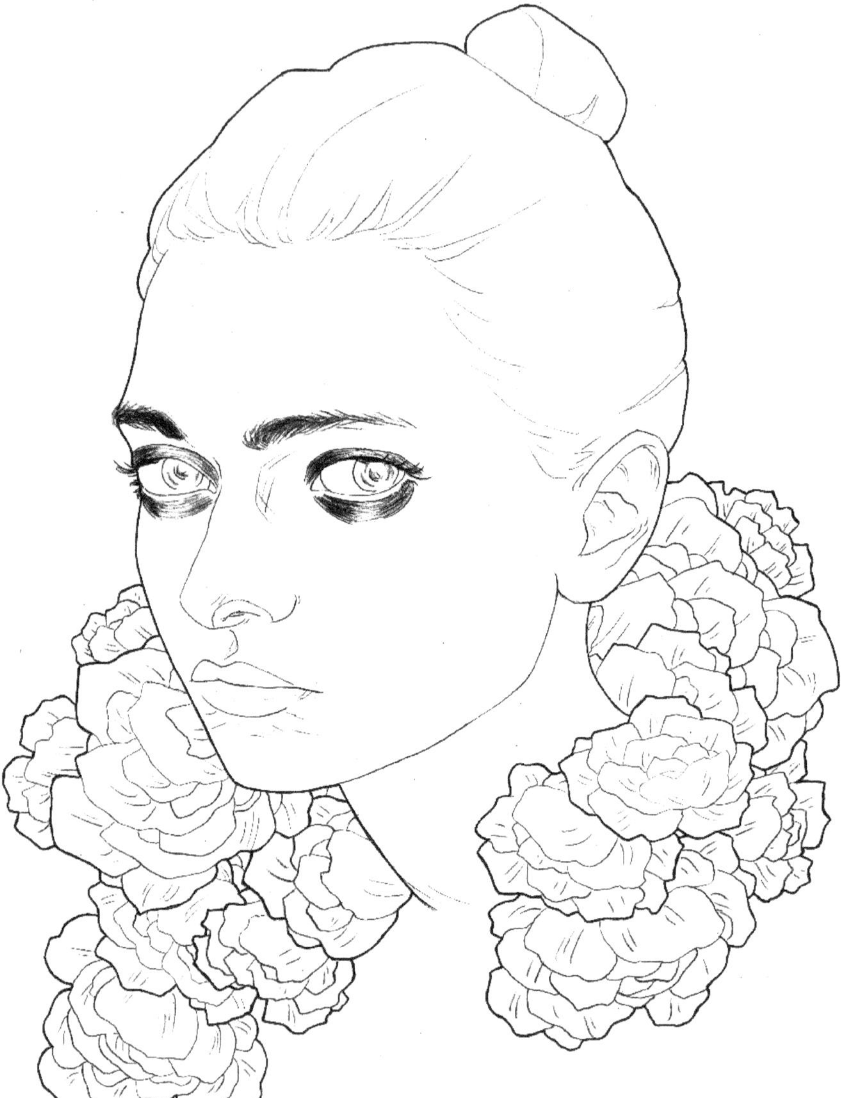

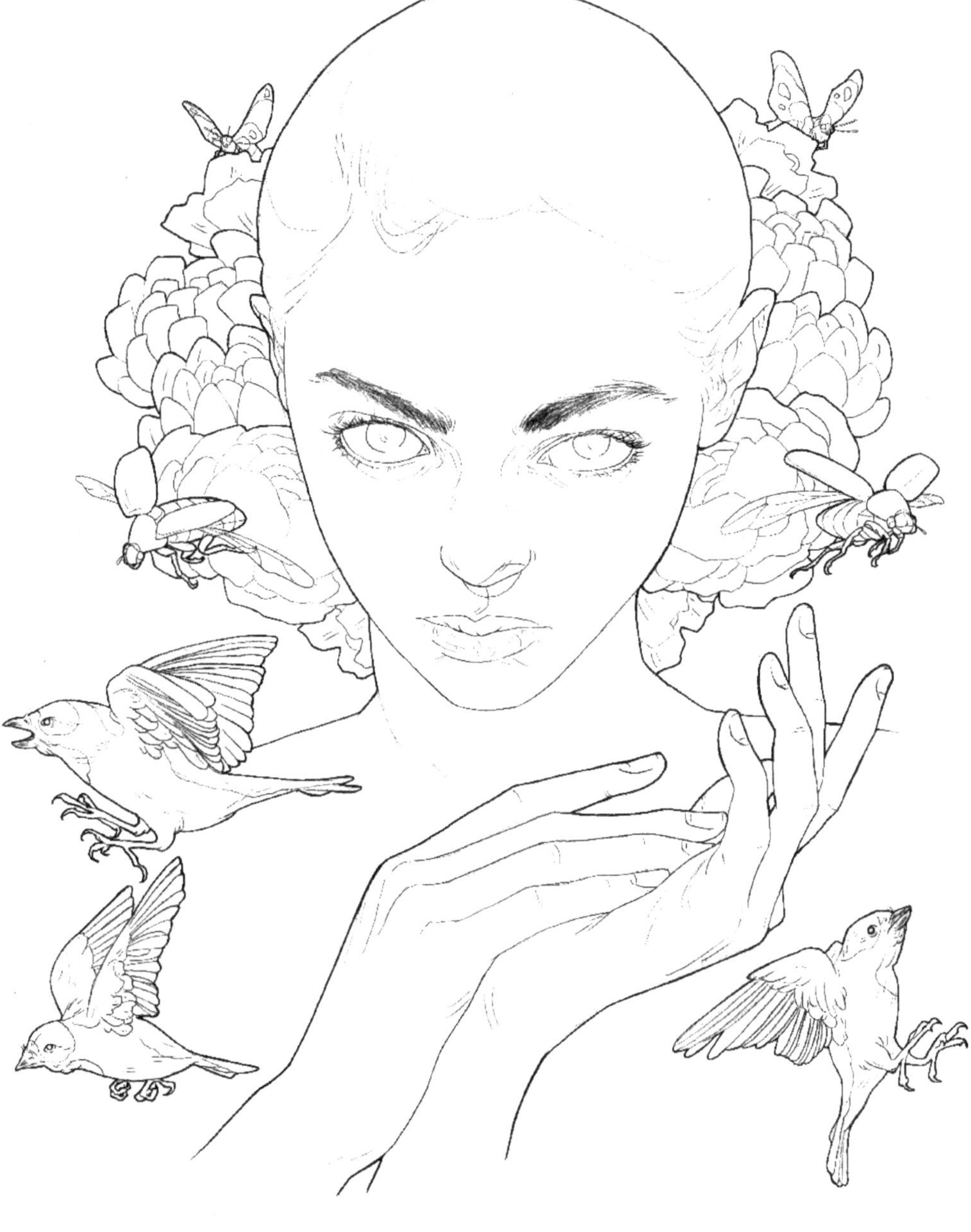

Figures

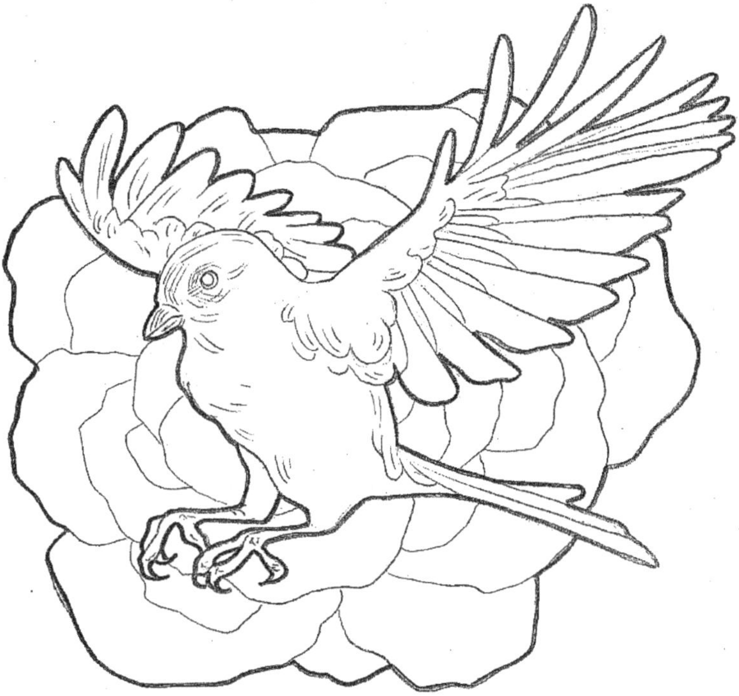

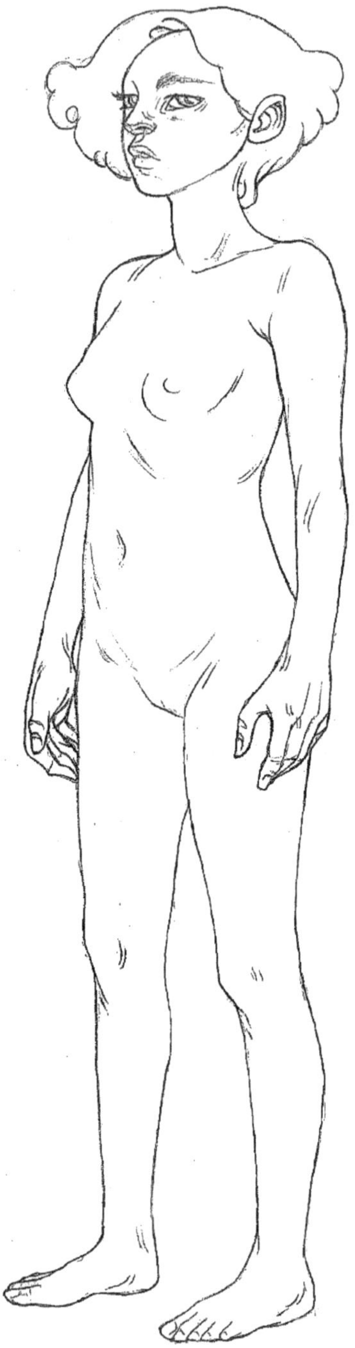

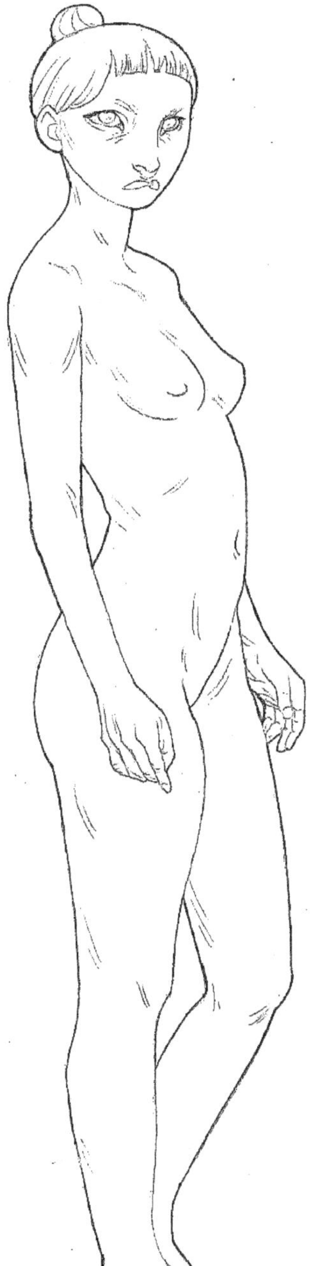

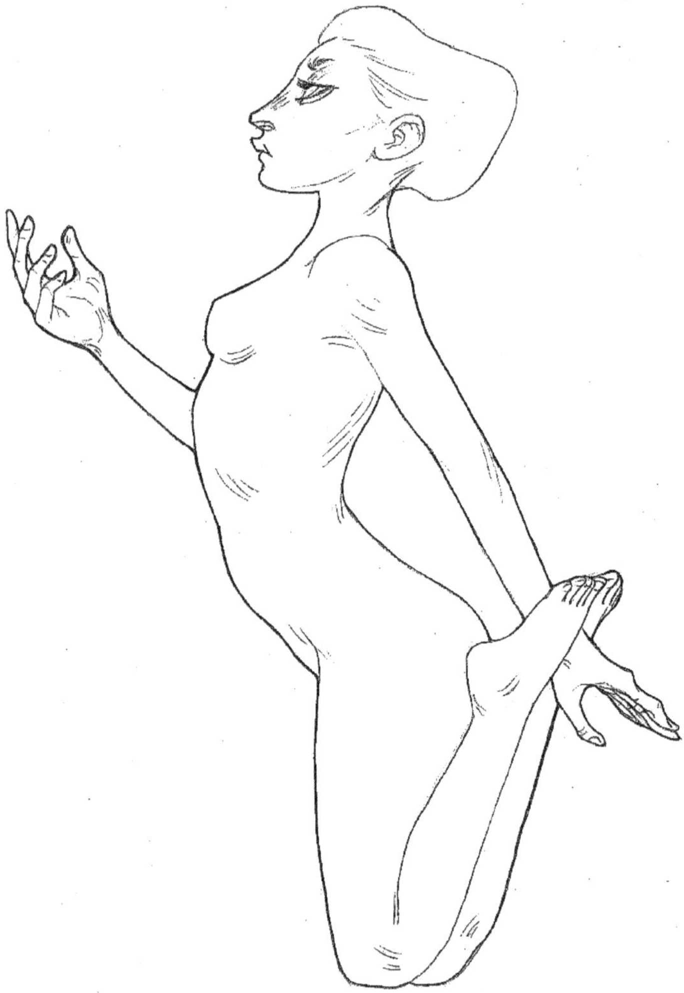

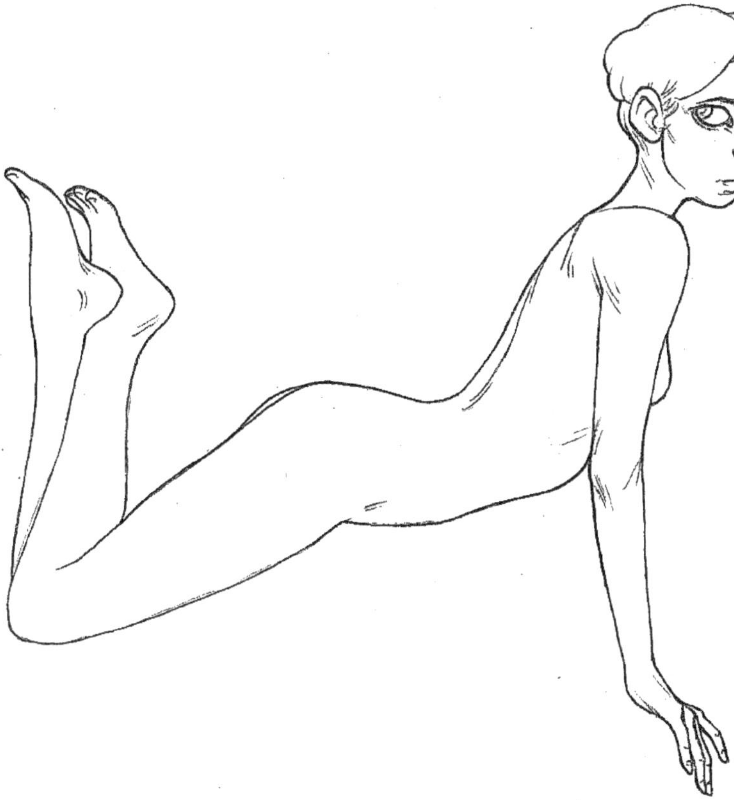

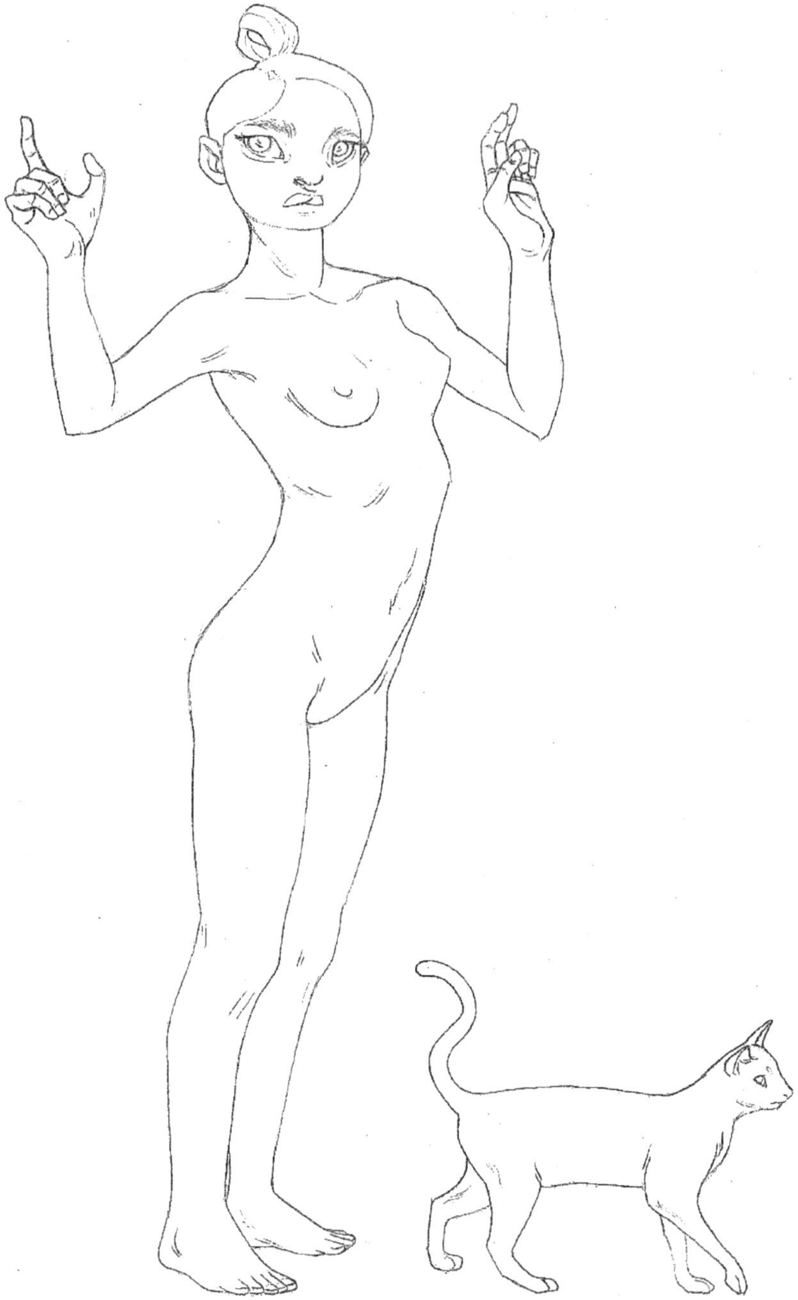

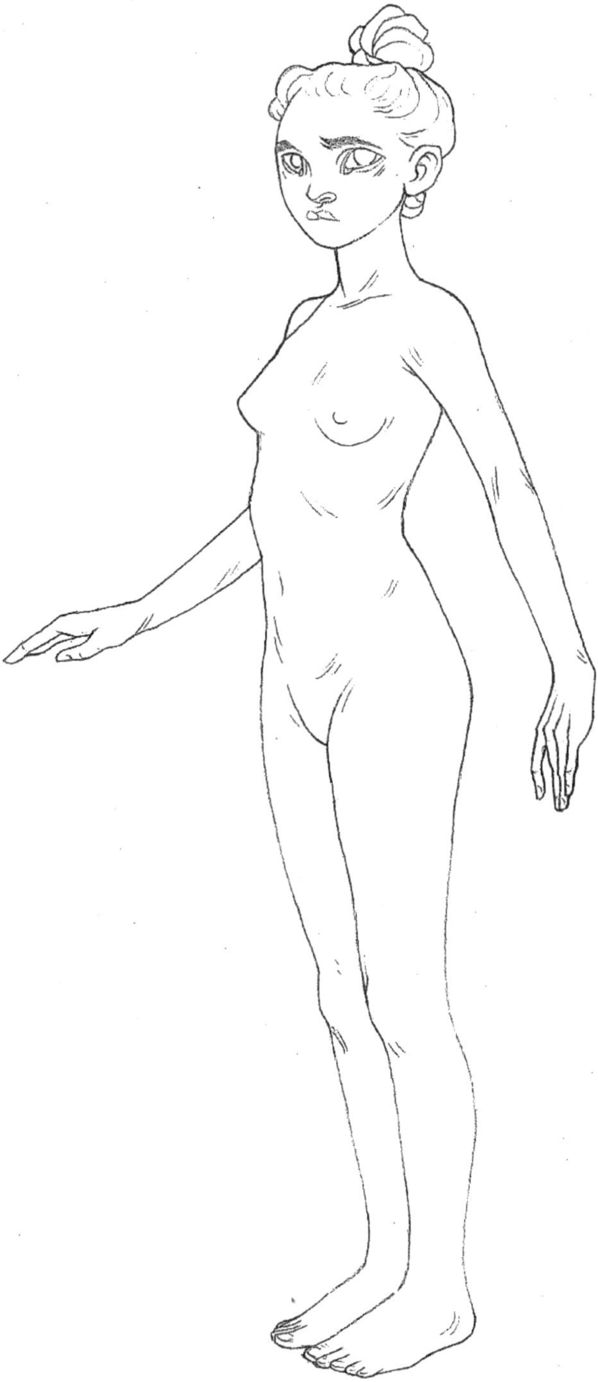

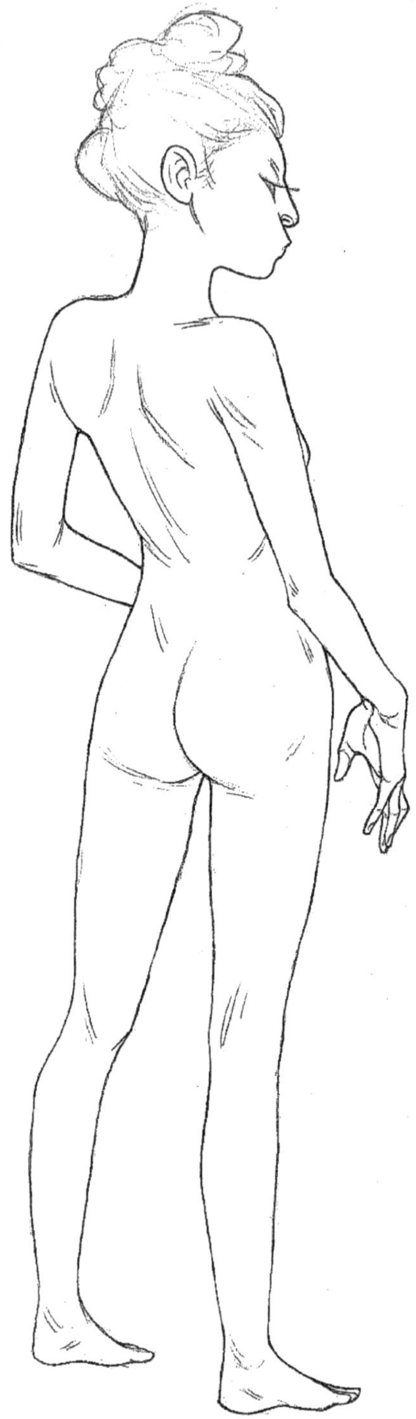

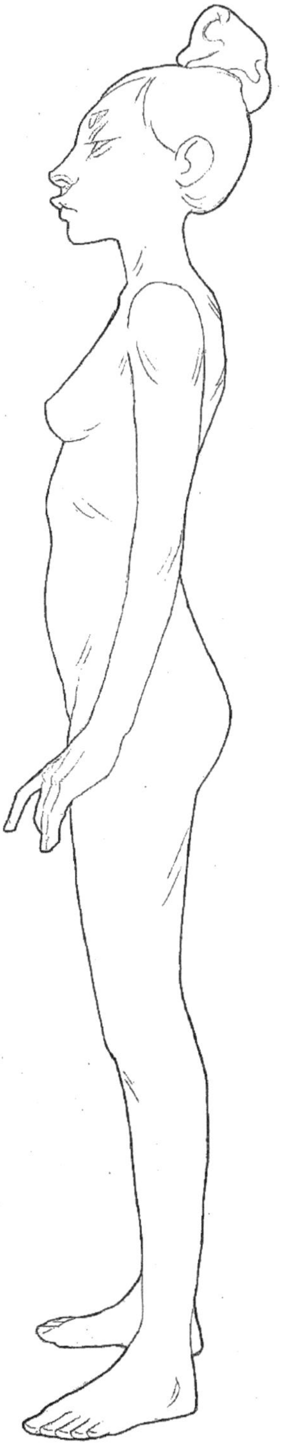

Section i. (Portraits)

vi. Sybil
vii. Duel
viii. Death-Head
ix. Crown-Bearer
x. Love
xi. Form
xii. Round
xiii. Emblem
xiv. Ink i
xv. Ink ii
xvi. Beetle
xvii. Damselfly
xviii. Alicia in Magnolia
xix. Gaze
xx. Nymph i
xxi. Nymph ii
xxii. Calamity
xxiii. Pardon
xxiv. .
xxv. Nymphaea
xxvi. Diamond
xxvii. Twin
xxviii. Bestow
xxix. Moths
xxx. Bloom
xxxi. Ancient Arbor

Section ii. (Figures)

www.ingramcontent.com/pod-product-compliance
Lightning Source LLC
Chambersburg PA
CBHW040817200526
45159CB00024B/3016
9780692865705